YOUR KNOWLEDGE HAS VALUE

Rosa Grieser

The cycle of culture, communication and identity

GRIN Verlag

Bibliografische Information der Deutschen Nationalbibliothek:

Die Deutsche Bibliothek verzeichnet diese Publikation in der Deutschen National-
bibliografie; detaillierte bibliografische Daten sind im Internet über http://dnb.d-
nb.de/ abrufbar.

Imprint:

Copyright © 2012 GRIN Verlag GmbH
Druck und Bindung: Books on Demand GmbH, Norderstedt Germany
ISBN: 978-3-656-40578-8

GRIN - Your knowledge has value

Der GRIN Verlag publiziert seit 1998 wissenschaftliche Arbeiten von Studenten, Hochschullehrern und anderen Akademikern als eBook und gedrucktes Buch. Die Verlagswebsite www.grin.com ist die ideale Plattform zur Veröffentlichung von Hausarbeiten, Abschlussarbeiten, wissenschaftlichen Aufsätzen, Dissertationen und Fachbüchern.

Visit us on the internet:

http://www.grin.com/

http://www.facebook.com/grincom

http://www.twitter.com/grin_com

The cycle of culture, communication and identity

When human beings are in the company of relatives, friends and neighbors, they might take it for granted that communication is a complex continuous process which has many nonverbal as well as verbal components. It is in the encounter with a stranger or being in a strange situation which inherent uncertainness. Having expectations how a stranger may act or how to act in a strange situation can help to reduce this uncertainness. These expectations are based on particular social convention, which are part of what is vague called culture (Payer: 2011). If a situation cannot meet the expectations, people become suddenly aware that, because all customary behaviors convey information, they struggle to understand the happening until they know the particular cultural code (Leach:1996:9p). A cultural code describes the system of representation by which signs and their meanings are arranged by cultural convention to temporarily stabilize significances in particular ways (Barker 2005: 436). Traffic lights are coded in a sequence: red for stop, orange for pause and green for go.

Language presents a system, in which human associate a certain sequence of letters with a world and a certain sequence of words as sentence. Moreover, every word has an agreed meaning for something even though the something might be an abstract such as a feeling, which human can only apprehend by knowing the particular cultural code (Culler: 1976: 36). Therefore language, as verbal communication, is constitutive of values, meaning and knowledge, it gives meaning to material objects and social practice, which are brought into view and made intelligible to human beings in terms which language delimits. (Barker 2005:88pp). Body language, as non-verbal communication, presents a customary convention that only can be understood if they are familiar. Nonverbal communication is a very comprehensive concept and there are many unconscious non-verbal behaviors that carry different meaning in different communities (Hall:2005:160).

Language as verbal or nonverbal communication is the medium in which cultural meanings are formed and communicated. Further is communication the means and medium through which we form knowledge about the social world and ourselves. According to this assumption communication, culture and identity are in a relationship between each other. This essay will embrace the elements which make up this connection, in order to discuss how communication, culture and identity form each other.

Bradford J. Hall points out that there are many definitions of culture which accent different aspects and some would be that overarching that culture becomes almost everything (Hall:2005:3).

Clifford Geertz claimed that his concept of culture '... is essentially a semiotic one. Believing, with Max Weber, that man is an animal suspended in webs of significance he himself has spun, I take culture to be those webs, and the analysis of it to be therefore not an experimental science in search of law but an interpretive one in search of meaning (Geertz:1973:5). Culture is here identified as meaning, which can only exist if someone else accepts that meaning. Geertz illustrates his idea with the example of blinking. Blinking can be seen as a movement of the eyelid, to recognize that it can be a secret motion to one's friend, requires the agreement about its meaning (Geertz:1999: 11p).

Similar to Geertz beforehand Bradford J. Hall emphasis the meaning and senses' culture '... as a historically shared system of symbolic resources through which we make our world meaningful" (Hall:2005:4). In this view, culture is a creation of a symbolic through which human decode actions in a way that they become meaningful (Hall:2005:8pp).

The idea of certain cultural codes was already used in Stuart Halls 'encoding/ decoding model' developed to describe communication as a process of transmitting a message from sender A to receiver B. In order to deliver information successfully A and B must use the same encoding and decoding system. Encoding and decoding are therefore fundamental processes in the communication exchange. The massage in the natural form must be encoded by the source and decoded by the receiver so that a symbolic exchange is produced. Consequently the 'meaning structure' of the sender cannot always be equal with the 'meaning structure' of the receiver. Understanding is then dependent upon the extent to which the decoded message is equivalent to the encoded message, and because the sender and the receiver occupy different positions in the communication process. The result is usually a distortion in communication (Hall: 1980:128pp.).

Bradford J. Hall surmise communication would refer to the generation of meaning. He claims that his definition would follow a "social constructive perspective in which meanings are generated through the interpretive practice of humans as they work out with each other the meanings of different messages."(Hall:2005:16). This interpretation process would not be narrowed to verbal face to face communication rather the process compasses every single moment in which meaning has been generated (Hall:2005.16).

Although the generated meaning differs between cultures, Hall discovered two features of communication which he defines as universal: interdependent and situational. According to him, everyone who is involved in a communication process influences each other's choices continually. This can even happen unconsciously and in silence. Choice refers in this coherence to the choice of response, for instance, responding angry, happy or disregardful. In Hall's perspective, it is very important to be aware of these choices, especially in the context of intercultural communication (Hall 2005: 17p.). Secondly, communication would always be situational, because it references to context. The same words might be used in a different context, through which they might generate a different meaning. For example, can the statement "that's great" describe something 'great' as well as it can be used in a sarcastic and angry context. These contextual features are differ between cultures, therefore they can only be understood in the native context (Hall:2005:19).

Moreover, Hall detect three key concepts in which culture is given form for conceiving the connection between communication and culture, which further provide tools 'for making sense of intercultural interaction'. These are worldviews, values and norms. Worldviews are described as very abstract beliefs about the way the world is, and are different within communities and cultures. Worldviews are used by human to understand any confusing behaviors in other culture groups (Hall:2005:31pp). Values would rather be an abstract concept than a belief, which reflect what is important to an individual or a group. Therefore "Values are grounded in beliefs about the way the world should be rather than assumptions about the way it is."(Hall:2005:49p.), and might be shared with members of other culture communities (Hall 2005:49pp). The third concept refers to norm, which are social rules that determine how people should act or not act (Hall:2005:52pp). Examples for norms are conversing protocols or a code of behavior.

Having regards to the connection between culture and communication, Hall identifies two perspectives: the monolithic forces and the reflexive force. The monopolistic force assumes first, that human behavior is based on a casual model, and second, that human interact in consistent, predictable ways (Hall:2005:56). The reflective force would again be based on two different assumptions. First, the relationship between communication and culture is not casual rather it is one of sense making. Worldviews, values and norm facilitate meaning, by helping to make sense of the surrounding world. Secondly is communication connected to culture forms in a situational moment and is not obligating for the entire community (Hall:2005:57p). Bradford J. Hall prefers the perspective of the reflective force as he presumes that this force exposed culture as a resource of communication without ignoring the importance of coherence and situation in the apprehension of interaction. Further this view would allow the relationship between culture and communication to have a certain pattern by being open to change, which would allow human to be active decision-makers who are explicable to social and cultural outcomes.

In the same way demonstrated Hall that there are some forms of communication which are universal for cultures. He claims that all human communities have narratives, which function as a teacher. Narratives explain, "… the way the world works, our place in the world, how to act in the world and how to evaluate the world around us." (Hall:2005:95). Another form which can be detected in every culture is rituals. In this context, rituals are customary observance, practice or pattern of behavior, which is regularly performed in a set manner. It is a structured sequence and can be a specific act of one's everyday lives. Rituals teach about values and relationships within a cultural community, as well as it provides a way for human to confirm their identity with those around them.

According to Hall, human would use the distinction of different identities and the expectation toward these to make their world meaningful. According to him "Identities are sets of social expectations related to ourselves and others that (a) are grounded in the interplay between similarities and difference and (b) pertain to the persona, relational and communal aspects of lives."(Hall: 2005:102). Hall illustrated the term 'expectation' on different roles we play, as an actor plays different roles in different movies. Caused by the way human-kind structure their world, people have different roles to play. Roles are determent for instance, by the profession, sex, peer group or age (Hall:2005:102pp). Another term for roles might be mask, as something what can be put on, changed or taken off. The mask a person is wearing determines expectations of other people towards that one's behavior, as well as that person has expectations about its own way to interact while wearing that mask. Further would human need to categorize other people in order to deal with the world around them, this can lead to stereotyping and the poor treatment of people.[1]

In view of the globalization, immigration and intercultural marriage, changing a role can imply for people with multi-cultural backgrounds to change in between nationalities (Samovar/Porter/McDaniel 2004:124). An in a western country living intercultural married couple from India and China might have adopted the lifestyle of the country they immigrated to; they play certain roles within this culture. Assuming their parents still live in India and China, they might change back into the set of roles associated with his originally culture background, when they are visiting their homelands.

---

[1] ethnocentrism and prejudice are other reasons why some prople are traded poortly (Hall: 2005: 191pp)

Jeffrey Weeks assumes that identity "...is about sameness and difference, about the personal and the social, about what you have in common with some people and what differentiates you from others"(Week:1990:89). Sharing the same idea Hall sees the heart of all identities in the "Interplay of similarity and difference" (Hall:2005:106). Similarity inasmuch as an adopted identity comprised something we share with others, for instance a nationality, profession or religion. On the other hand, can a similarity abnegate another identity, an adult is not a child, and a pupil is not a teacher.

Identity concerns both the self-identity and the social or cultural identity. Hence identity is always about the personal and social, about one's self and the relation to others. Therefore, culture is expressed through humans identity as well as one's identity is a product of culture and cannot exist outside its representation and can only be understood of in its context.

Moreover assumes Hall, that identity is connected to communication in two ways: 1. Communication is a reflection of our identity. 2. Communication constitutes our identity (Hall 2005:113pp.). The reflective way refers to the role expectation or identity labels and is "... based on the common idea that people's actions will reflect their identity."(Hall 2005:113). While the reflective way is to be predicated on the assumption that identity is consistent, a German person will always be a German person, the constitutive way provided that identity is rather a process than a static. While a person is going through life, it might change certain identities, as for example by switching in between two peer groups or professions; identity in this context is rather "something we do …than something we inherently are" (Hall 2005:115).

Hence communication is a reflection of one's identity but in the same way communication constitutes one's identity. However, both perspectives would be in Hall's opinion insufficient by themselves; it is only in the viewpoint which takes both perspectives into account that issues, which arise out of identity apprehensions can be understood (Hall:2005:117).

Hall figures that identity is an important fact of communication, as every inter-action is based on verbal or non-verbal interaction (Hall:2005:102), and there-fore a source of misunderstandings. Being aware of which kinds of actions are appropriated in which context is part of our cultural knowledge and is not necessarily the same in every cultural community (Hall:2005:132). Mohan and his associated give examples of customs of different cultures, which are often perplexing to a person of another culture background. They tell the story of Spanish girl who had a chinese friend, who did not mind burping and farting in front of her. As this sort of behavior is considered rude in her culture she felt offended. Trying to find the right words to explain this to her friend, she started shaking her legs, which on the other hand is considered rude in the Chinese culture (Mohan/MC Gregor/Sanders/Archee:2008:104).

Another source of misunderstanding is what John Gumperz called 'cross-talk' which is grounded in different cultural conventions related to our verbal communication. The basis of verbal communication is as already discussed language. Considering assumptions on a contextual level, is according to Hall a useful way to find an explanation of misunderstanding in verbal communication (Hall:2005:132). He figures that human beings are always mired in cultural webs that frame what is expected and appropriated in a certain context, and conflicts might often be the consequence of framing a situation differently. By being aware of these 'frame expectations', people can accustom themselves to recognize cultural difference which otherwise might be missed (Hall:2005:132pp). Another area of intercultural misunderstanding is the verbal structure and content of cultural communities. He refers in this term to language, the use of words and the use of words, which are not taken literally. (Hall:2005:139pp).

Further might intercultural misunderstandings be rooted in the non-verbal conversation process, which is not dependent on verbal communication but closely related. Human use non-verbal language to underline their verbal messages or the body language might be a contradiction to what a person just said. Further verbal- and non-verbal communication are related through what Hall calls 'Substitution', for instance rolling of eyes, 'Accentuation', to increase the meaning, 'Complement' to modify a verbal message and 'Regulation', which changes the flow of a conversation by, for example, nodding one's head in order to encourage someone to go ahead (Hall 2005:161p).

In Hall's assumption, there are three types of non-verbal communication: Kinesics, such as facial expressions and gestures; Proxemics which describes the use of space to another person; and Paralanguage, which directly accompanies our verbal communication through laughter or volume. Which kind of body language is seen as appropriated and non-offended differs from culture to culture and it is important to be capable of to notice the acceptability of different ways of doing things.

In regard to the relationship of culture, communication and identity, it has been pointed out that culture is a creation of a symbolic through which human decode actions to make them meaningful. Culture is an instance which is expressed and learned through communication. Further would communication as well refer to 'generated meaning' (Hall: 2005:16p). The way how a person communicates, which kind of communication is considered as appropriate, the use of verbal as well as non-verbal language is learned through the culture a person is raised in. Hall proofed that the connection between culture and communication is one of sense making and human use worldviews, values and norm as facilitate meaning in order to do so. Additionally, communication connected to culture forms in a situational moment. Culture can be seen as a source of communication, which allows the relationship between culture and communication to be open to change. Although cultures might differ significantly from each other, Hall recognized Narratives and Rituals as universal communication forms, which offer human a way to confirm their identity with those around them. Identity is connected to meaning, as human use the distinction of different identities and expectations to make sense of their world. Further culture is expressed through human's identity as well as one's identity is a product of culture. Moreover, is communication a reflection and constitution of one's identity. Culture, communication and identity are therefore used by human beings to 'make their world meaningful.

In this context, all conflicts of intercultural communication refer to different codes, used to make one's world meaningful, such as the meaning of objects, relationships, and how values, norms and ideals are arranged. In order to solve or avoid these conflicts is to create the right situation, a positive communication in which any contact happens. Another important element is the

ability to forgive people who might have seemed to offend (Hall:2005:226pp).

In context of intercultural travels does that mean that people need to be able

to acculturate in order to meet their needs. Acculturation does not mean as-

similation; it refers more to the procedure of becoming communicatively ca-

pable in a culture someone has not been raised in (Hall:2005:267pp). Being

in a strange culture demands to learn and internalize the different meanings

and sense making structures of culture, communication and identity within a

particular cultural community.

References

Baker, Chris, 2005, 'Culture Studies. Theory and Practice', SAGA Publications,
London, United Kingdom.

Culler, Jonathan, 1976, ´Sausure´, Havester Press, London, United Kingdom.

Geertz, Clifford, 1999, ´Dichte Beschreibung: Beitraege zum Verstehen kultureller Systeme´. 6. Ed. Suhrkamp Verlag. Frankfurt a. Main. Germany.

Geertz, Clifford,1973, ´The interpretation of cultures´,Suhrkamp
Verlag.Frankfurt am Main, Germany.

Hall, Bradford J., 2005 'Among Cultures. The Challenge of Communication',
2.Ed., Wadsworth, Belmont, United States of America.

Hall, Stuart, 1980, 'Encoding/Decoding' In: 'Culture, Media, Language', Ed.
Stuart Hall et.al., Routledge. New York. United States of America.128-138.

Leach, Edmund R., 1996,´Culture and Communication. The logic by which
symbols are connected.´ Cambridge University Press. Cambridge. United
Kingdom

Mohan, T., MC Gregor, H., Sanders, S., Archee, R.,2008, 'Communicating as
Professionals. Thomson, Victoria, Australia.

Payer, Margarete, 2011, ´ Internationale Kommunikationskulturen. Kultur und Kommunikation.´viewed at 24.05.12

http://www.payer.de/kommkulturen/kultur02.htm.

Samovar, L., Porter R., McDaniel, E., 2004, 'Communication Between Cultures'. Thomson Wadsworth, United States of America.

Week, Jeffrey, 1990, 'The Value of Difference'. In: Identity: Community, Culture, Difference. Ed. J. Rutherford, Lawrence&Wishart. London, United Kingdom.